Making Friends with C

Introducing Children to M

A Colouring Workbook

By Caroline Sherwood

Illustrations by Alixandra Marschani

GREEN MAGIC

GREEN MAGIC
Seed Factory
Aller
Langport
Somerset
TA10 0QN
England
www.greenmagicpublishing.com

ISBN 9781838418540

Designed & typeset by CARRIGBOY, Wells, Somerset.
www.carrigboy.co.uk

This book is dedicated
to the Unborn Potential
which draws us Home
and which moves
to express Itself
through us.

Caroline Sherwood

To the children I have taught,
now teach, and
those yet to come...

Alixandra Marschani

Thank You

- To all my Teachers: physical and non-physical.
- To all the people (some of whom are no longer with us in physical form) who, over the decades, have supported the various magical manifestations of this little book: Dian Booth, Fiona Carnie, Simon Cook, Emőke Csiki, Glynis Dallas-Chapman, Ruth Griffiths, Chris Harbon, Anne Hassett, Sarah Hyde, Daniel Kronenberg, Carolyn Litchfield, Daniela Marin, Norma Mariouw-Smit Guise, Chris Marshall, Joanna May, Pamela Moolman, Ian Murray, Virág-Lilla Rácz, Kevin Redpath, Ngak'chang Rinpoche, Liz Seelbach, Solveig Taylor, Susanna Vermaase, Nigel Walker and Sean Williams.

Foreword

Children are the young of the human species and as such are learning to be adults – but what kind of adults can they become? It should be possible that we have more choice than other species of creatures – but although we see a variety of choices represented in the adults our children become; these choices are somewhat illusory. As adult humans, we labour under the illusion that we are free to make choices – but the choices we have, are mainly those we are given. Although these given choices appear to be different – they are mainly different versions of the same programming. This is not the way it has to be.

I have known Caroline Sherwood – as a friend – since 1986. She is one of a small number of people I have met in my life who have sought to undermine and expose the conditioning we all accept – and has had success in that endeavour. Anyone who moves beyond their condition is naturally impelled to facilitate others to experience the freedom of their own individuality – and this she has done. Caroline has influenced many people in her life – but not in the obvious way. You will not find her as a prominent figure on the worldwide workshop circuits – nor does she have a growing spiritual community who follow her guidance. These things are only marks of spiritual success for those who take them to be so.

Although we live at a time where the cult of the individual is paramount – many people seem to understand individuality merely as 'self orientation' or 'self obsession'. Spirituality is often seen as the cure for self orientation – but usually at the expense of individuality – and therefore individuality tends to be regarded with suspicion by those who applaud conventional spiritual values.

The fact of the matter is that we *are* individuals; or rather, that we can become individuals – but not by trying to be different. Many people mistake individuality for ostentation, pretension, affectation, flamboyance, posturing or quirkiness. Authentic individuality may bear some passing resemblance to these traits – but it is without compulsion and no effect is sought. Freedom is not necessarily the casting off of societal mores or the assumption of an unconventional or eccentric lifestyle – but the recognition of conditioning in oneself. Authentic freedom is the ability to make decisions on the basis of what is discovered to be the real condition of the world.

Caroline Sherwood has offered a wonderful possibility in her book – as it provides 'experiential contexts' in which freedom can be discovered. Meditation is a word that has many meanings according to tradition – but whatever the tradition, the essential theme is the discovery of freedom. It is hard to teach children the nature of freedom – because we often impose our own versions of freedom upon them. The only way to discover freedom is to discover it for oneself and this book is a key to that discovery.

Children are more astute than most people imagine – and although their attention span can be shorter than that of adults, they can become intensely absorbed under the right conditions. Caroline has provided such conditions with the experiential contexts suggested in her book – and I feel confident than any child would respond cheerfully and inquisitively to what is presented here.

Ngak'chang Rinpoche
Lineage Lama (principal teacher of the Aro,
within the Nyingma tradition
of Tibetan Buddhism)

Introduction

This book has been through a number of previous incarnations. Five years elapsed between writing the first edition and its publication in 1995. It literally dropped into my mind in its entirety during an afternoon's walk 'round the block,' over stream and down track in the Somerset village of Stoney Stratton where I was living. It arranged itself in its basic form on the page within one hour of returning home.

Then began the lengthy process of locating and liaising with an illustrator (I did not meet Susanna Masheder until after the book got into print - it was all done by telephone and letter); approaching publishers, getting turned down, making contacts and finally plucking up the courage to self-publish; followed by months of learning to do just that - from library books!

Since the first edition came out, I have been through many changes and a deepening of my understanding about the value and purpose of meditation and spiritual life in general and this is reflected to some extent in the additional exercises in the second edition.

Thanks to a handful of enthusiastic non-professional distributors (all friends and acquaintances), the first edition found its way as far afield as Hong Kong, Australia and the United States, as well as all over Britain.

Once the first edition had sold out, the project went quiet for a while, though many friends were encouraging me to bring out a second. I was sure that if this was to appear, it had to be professionally published. Interesting and challenging as it was to self-publish, I had

to teach myself three skills from scratch – publishing, marketing and distribution; and I didn't want to do this again.

When I met Alixandra Marschani in Glastonbury, it was a signal that the time had come to resurrect the project. It was too much of a 'coincidence' to find, combined in one talented soul; a practising meditator, a painter engaged with sacred art and a primary school teacher!

Then, a series of unexpected connections led to a new Hungarian edition being published in Romania, which took me to Transylvania for a couple of book fairs and workshops. This was followed by a Romanian edition.

It was another fortuitous meeting with Peter Gotto in Labyrinth Books in Glastonbury High Street, followed by an intuitive 'nudge' received on the 376 bus on my way home, which prompted me to contact Green Magic Publishing; so the Spirit of Avalon must also be acknowledged as having played a part in this project.

It seems that I am sometimes ahead of my time and this is now an idea whose time *has* really come. So I offer this third English incarnation of the book at a time when the value and relevance of material of this kind are becoming recognized and more widely appreciated. I trust it will sow beneficial seeds for the future in many minds, both young and old.

Caroline Sherwood
Cheltenham, 2021

Contents

What this Book's About

Sometimes we're so busy chattering away to ourselves in our head that we don't notice how quiet it is underneath. We forget to feel how good it feels inside – how good it is to be ALIVE. Sometimes we forget for so long that we tie ourselves up in knots and then things start to feel uncomfortable.

Most of the time, we're doing things or learning things – or talking. But it's also important to know what's going on **inside** us as well as around us. This is how we start to make friends with ourselves.

Have you heard of meditation? Maybe you know some grown-ups who meditate, or who go to classes – maybe your parents do? Well – meditation is a complicated word for making friends with ourselves, by learning to listen to the beautiful silence inside us.

If you get a notebook and a drawing pad to go with this book, you can put down anything special that you notice or anything you want to remember that happens while you do the exercises. This book is set out so that your teacher can read the exercises out to a class. Some of them you can try with one other person or a group of friends. You can always try all of them on your own as well.

Sometimes there is a little number above a word, like this: [2]. This means that there is a note for the teacher at the end of the page (a footnote). I have put it there, because I thought it might be more interesting for your teacher than for you, but of course you can read it if you want to!

There are many wonderful things you can do to get to know yourself better and to become really good friends with yourself. In fact, everything we do can become part of our project. This book is here to help you to make a start.

For the Grown-Ups

I have no children, but I am able to remember, very clearly, what it felt like to be a child. How much simpler my life might have been had I been offered real spiritual guidance earlier! By real spiritual guidance, I mean effective *methods* which cultivate what is good and true in us and which dissolve the suffering and discontent which we have inherited and which we reinforce by ignorance of any alternative. In my childhood days, I had to make what sense I could of *Churchianity* (I always had a lot of time for Jesus, whom I experienced as a wonderful, wild healing fire), until my search led me (at the age of twenty-two, after a year of psychotherapy) to a meditation teacher.

It was the summer of 1973 and the place was southwest France. I was attending a humanistic psychology gathering. Wearied and intimidated by the plethora of negative and emotionally-indulgent workshops, I responded to a little notice in the dining room: MEDITATION ON THE GRASS AT 10 p.m. BRING A BLANKET. I turned up and sat at the back in the dark, hunched awkwardly under my blanket on the sloping lawn, straining to follow the teacher's instructions. The teacher was John Garrie, and, as his closing words: "Peace to all beings, may all beings be well and happy – and free from fear"[1] drifted to me out of the darkness, they were accompanied by waves of pale, blue energy which suffused and stilled me. I knew I had found what I had been unconsciously thirsting for, and although I did not know it for several months, that moment marked the beginning of a seven year training in Satipatthāna-Vipassanā (mindfulness-insight).[2] During that seven years, students came from far and wide to that gifted and compassionate man – they learnt, for the first time in their lives, to relax their bodies, to untangle their confusions and to heal deep wounds.

Back in England, during my first teaching session with John Garrie, a fly landed on my arm. I slapped at it absent mindedly. "Don't do that!" he snapped. "But I don't like flies," I whined. "Is that any reason to kill them?" he asked. My first conscious lesson in compassion and the inter-connectedness of life was thus delivered.

John Garrie was a remarkable teacher. Finding himself with clairvoyant gifts before such things were well-known or fashionable, he had no choice but to train in spiritualist circles. He became an actor and even developed his own skating clown – Bluenose. He worked as a charismatic healer; restoring speech to the dumb and breaking crutches over his knees as the 'lame' walked freely down the steps from the stage into the hall.

In the late 1950s, Buddhist monks began coming to Europe from the Far East. John met such a monk (from Burma) and began his meditation training. Immediately his psychic

---

[1] See dedication prayer on page 85.
[2] *Satipatthāna* has been described as the 'heart' of Buddhist meditation. It is the fundamental practice of mindfulness which Sakyamuni Buddha recommended to his earliest followers. It has four foundations 1) mindfulness (or awareness) of body, 2) mindfulness of feeling, 3) mindfulness of mind, 4) mindfulness of mental object (what the attention is focused on in any moment).

gifts deserted him. They were actually only changing form and undergoing a period of purification, as he moved deeper in his new practice.

In the healing days, people had often reported seeing seven-foot Zulus, and the like, standing behind him as he healed. He never believed a word of it! Not that he doubted the perceptions of the audience, but rather he gave no credence to their explanations for what they were seeing, nor empowered them with any special significance. This insistence on ruthless precision and clarity of interpretation was something that John Garrie imparted to me. He developed in me what I have come to refer to colloquially as "a well-developed nose for nonsense!"

John explained to me that, in the early days, he was "used" by his psychic gifts, because he was unconscious of their nature and origin. Later, and certainly by the time I knew him, his considerable healing ability was flowing again, but now almost casually – well-integrated with everything else he did and certainly subservient to his primary work of teaching students to become responsible for their own abilities and health. John often said, "I'm not giving you bunches of flowers; I'm giving you packets of seeds." Today, over 40 years later, those seeds continue to produce fresh green shoots.

Grace, wisdom, inspiration and instruction have continued to pour into my life since those early days, through many teachers, and the full story of that is recorded in my memoir, *Following a Thread of Gold*.

As a child, I remember especially valuing the people who could take me beyond myself – those who could expand my view, inspire my imagination or enthusiasm – those who communicated love, justice and nobility in how they lived or what they said. These were the people who offered a gap in the plodding mundanity of school life. There were few such people, but two drama teachers stood out amongst them.

I remember Frieda Hodgson. She was the best sort of English eccentric – handsome, uncompromising and totally dedicated. Her cheeks were chiseled and never bore a trace of make up; her nose was large, hooked and strong. She had ice-grey eyes which were at the same time liquid and piercing – they never missed a trick. Her bosom, which was truly shelf-like, was usually swathed in a black velvet dress, complete with cream ruff and cuffs. Her silver hair encircled her head in a coil and a flat, Elizabethan-style black, velvet hat, worn at an angle, completed the romantic appearance.

She was 70 when I had the remarkable good fortune of having her as my teacher, and had been teaching drama for 50 years. She would coax, cajole, encourage and praise through the roof when we were good, and fly into displays of disgust when we were mediocre. During rehearsals, she would stand at the back of the hall, booming: *"Bigger, darling, BIGGER!"* when I mumbled; or: *"Caroline Sherwood, I don't believe you!"* when I wasn't putting my heart and soul into it. She accepted nothing but the best from her students and she knew our best was way beyond the limits we had settled on.

Every Christmas we had a 'speech recital' in the school library, fragrant with a Christmas tree and lit only by flickering firelight, the sparkle of the tree and candles. Mrs Hodgson would sit at one side, completely absorbed in the absorption of her students. Her face would change with the moving moods of the pieces we were performing. Sometimes she seemed even ecstatic, head held back and high; eyes closed. Now – more than half a century later – I can still remember her phone number. I used to ring her for discussions, suggestions and moral support before speech exams. Often, she would ask me to run through my piece over the phone, and her advice was: *Walk with it, wash in it, eat it… Live it and breathe it.*

My last drama teacher before university was Gwendoline James. She was as cheese to chalk, compared with Mrs Hodgson, but I learnt many and different things from her too. She was petite, neat, and femininely elegant. She wore pastel colours, high heels with ankle straps, false eyelashes and immaculately applied make-up. A very fine spangled hairnet twinkled on her wavy, piled-high, golden hair. She taught speech, drama and ballroom dancing and was an oasis of inspiration to me in my darker boarding school days.

She once asked me to "speak for two minutes on cream buns" (I was amazed how much there was to say about cream buns!) and to address the rest of the class as if I were a piano in the corner of the room (which I found incredibly difficult). She got some good work out of me, such that on one occasion my parents didn't recognize me for the first couple of minutes in my leading role as Cuthman in Christopher Fry's, *The Boy with a Cart.*

Mother Deagle was in charge of my class for a year at the Sacred Heart Convent in Hammersmith, London. She was a dignified lady, who had an aura of sober and genuine authority, a strongly musical streak and a twinkling sense of humour. The class would fall silent when she crossed the threshold, but not out of fear – simply because of the strength of her calm and steady presence. Regularly, at the beginning of her lessons, she would ask us to rest our heads on our arms on the desk and to close our eyes. She would then read a poem or a prayer or passage of gently philosophical prose. In so doing, she quietened us and cleared our minds in readiness for her lesson. I loved those sessions – a blessed chance to come to stillness amid the scrabble of school life.

It was my passionate interest in what makes people 'tick', as well as growing up in a theatrical family, that gave me my initial love of drama and it was through my love of theatre that I eventually discovered an interest in psychology and, later, in meditation. My earliest performance was as a shepherd in the junior school's Nativity play. I worked for weeks on my opening line: "The m…ooon is rising!" And when the moment came, the walls fell away and I could see that first century moon shining down from the star-spangled midnight Bethlehem sky and hear the snuffle of the sheep.

So, from a very young age, I knew that there was a space in me which, when I entered it consciously, contained the potential for endless possibilities. Later, giving a convincing performance of a 60 year old when I was nineteen, fired in me a burning need not so much to perform any more, but to find out who and what I actually was. It was then only a year's short step from drama to meditation.

Meditation

My earliest memory of meditative activity was during the school's morning radio broadcasts. I must have been about eight. We had to curl up on the floor and imagine ourselves as tiny seeds, beginning to grow. It was magical and refreshing for me to use my imagination in this way and that early inspiration forms the basis for the *Making Friends with My Body* section in this book.

There were books in my childhood which also served to awaken a sense of the spiritual in me. The first was, *At the Feet of the Master*, by Krishnamurti (under his earlier name of Alcyone). I can't have been more than ten when I discovered it among my father's books. As I read it, something in me turned inside out. It was published in Madras by the Theosophist Office in 1912 and, despite its tattiness and rather archaic language; I treasured it as one might a gold thread that leads to the heart of the labyrinth.

It was my first taste of spiritual teachings and it made my heart dance. After my father's death, it joined my collection and, later, with its leather-bound, gold-embossed binding expertly restored, I presented it as a gift to the Australian-born teacher and master, Barry Long, who was recognized by many as one of Krishnamurti's successors in the West. [3]

Before I go any further, it might be useful to explain my use of the word '*meditation*'. Although it is often used to refer to practices which are thousands of years old, the word did not appear in the English language until the middle of the sixteenth century. Since then, it has been adopted by many people to mean many things. In ancient languages, such as Sanskrit and Tibetan, there is a rich and highly technical vocabulary which very precisely describes the deepest nature of a human being and a wide range of spiritual practices, all of which have become encapsulated under the one English word; meditation. So, if we are to be precise in our definition of what it means to meditate, we need many words. It is easier to say what it isn't!

According to dictionary definitions and in everyday speech, meditation is associated with reflection, contemplation and discursive thought and is likened to pondering or musing over a given topic or theme. To this definition has been added the activities of prayer, visualization and guided fantasy. In this book, the word meditation refers to none of these. I am using the word to refer to a more original and fundamental practice; namely the observation of ourselves as we actually are. Not as we believe or think that we are; nor as we would like to be or have been told we are by others. This practice of simple awareness forms part of a wider discipline, which is the cultivation of our full human potential through the awakening of our spiritual nature.

We can apply our physical and mental faculties to all the activities to which I have referred, but the act of meditation is to shine the light of attention onto these faculties themselves – to turn the attention, as it were, away from the flickering images on the screen before the eyes, back into the projector itself. It is a matter of bringing awareness to bear on all aspects of our being and lives. In so meditating, we are not adding anything

---

[3] His book on Meditation is the best introduction for adults that I know of in English.

to ourselves and not even seeking answers to our problems and questions in any *experience* or *activity*. Rather, we are observing ourselves and our situation as they are and we are revealing ourselves to ourselves through a process of gradual unfoldment or unveiling. The fruits of such focused attention are an increase in self-understanding and of the greater reality within which we live our lives. Such meditation also releases in us dormant abilities and potentials and allows them a new and creative space within which to flower. It improves clarity, concentration, memory and efficiency, and it calls forth kindness, compassion and insight. As my teacher, John Garrie, used to say: "We learn to do the ordinary in a brilliant way."

The exercises in this book spring from time-tested methods, rendered anew with children in mind. Many of them derive from ancient methods of Insight Meditation and Tibetan Buddhist methods which I have studied and practised. I am deeply indebted to both Christianity and Buddhism, but I espouse no religion, as it is my understanding that *spirituality* is of more relevance to our times than is religion. It may be useful to remember that the Buddha wasn't a *Buddh-ist* (in fact the concept would have been alien to his teaching), and Jesus of Nazareth certainly wasn't a *Christ-ian*.

The truth precedes all religions and has expressed itself in many forms throughout history. So, though rooted in tradition, this book does not seek to promote any particular dogma or doctrine and is suitable for people of all creeds, faiths and backgrounds. I purposely offer no philosophy, as it is my aim to encourage the direct knowledge which comes from self-observation, and not thinking or conceptualization.

Meditation for Children

The exercises cover all aspects of a child's life – the use of the senses and the perceptive faculty – and they include the opportunity to develop qualities such as stillness, observation, concentration, consideration and sensitivity. If practised carefully, they can lead to valuable new ways of perceiving and being in the world.

The exercises can also be used as a basis for other work and play – for conversation and discussions about spiritual matters, for story-writing, drawing, painting, singing, drama and exploring nature.

Each exercise has a specific purpose, designed to focus on a particular facet of being or experience. I have included a guiding note with each one, as well as offering suggestions for further activities.

The material (which is intended particularly for children of seven to eleven years old) will be most effective if it is introduced by adults whom the children respect and trust and if it is presented one-to-one or in small groups.

Having said that, I have received feedback from several adults saying things like, "Never mind about children, *I* need to use this book!" So, let's say that I hope it can work as a book for the young at heart of all ages. Of course, if you are a teacher, once you are familiar with the exercises, you will be able to adapt them to suit the age group you are working with.

Spiritual Life for Children – The Natural Way

Spiritual does not mean adhering to any religious formula, nor does it mean cultic or exclusive. The word spirit comes from the Latin *spiritus* which means *breath*. To be spiritual is to be one with the breath of life. To educate in the spirit is to encourage full *respiration* (which is comprised of complete in-spiration, and complete ex-piration) – both physically and psychologically; by 'leading forth' the essential nature and inborn gifts of the child.

A spiritual education is an education which is in harmony with the natural way of things. It emphasizes quality of being, rather than acquisition of information. Such an education recognizes, acknowledges and seeks to nurture the innate goodness and beauty of the child's being – in the first place to maintain his or her connection to immortality, and secondly to prevent the development of an emotional and unhappy personality. Like all good healthcare, spiritual life is holistic and preventative. It nourishes the best, so that disease has no basis in which to establish itself.

It is the serious and delightful responsibility of adults and parents to introduce children to a spiritual view from the very first. To *educate* means to lead forth (the innate abilities of the student; from the Latin *ex* – out of + *ducare* – to lead) and not to stuff full of information, facts or knowledge, divorced from the wisdom and personal development of the child: which allows one to use what is known wisely and to discriminate what is worth knowing from what is not. Over the years I have noticed that people who are quite devoted to living a spiritual life are often at a loss as to how to communicate the *essence* of what they value to their children. I hope this book may provide some inspiration and nourishment in this area.

A newborn baby is an expression of the timeless in form. So, if a baby is a reflection of perfection, what happens between then and the age of five or six – when we see a grouchy, snotty-nosed, tear-stained, argumentative brat dragging round the supermarket behind her mother? Personality happens – the creeping development of emotional personality happens. And where does this come from? It is partly inherited and partly learned by example and imitation. The child learns how to behave by copying the adults – not necessarily their overt behaviour, but their prevalent mood, style and energy.

I spent much of my childhood having tantrums: discontented, demanding, ungrateful. I felt something was missing. It was not until I entered therapy at the age of 21 that I even began to look at this and not until I started to meditate a year later that I began to unravel it. There are memories of great beauty and completeness in my childhood, as well as memories of degradation and pain. Memories such as herding the cows with my friend on a Somerset farm where we had gone for a holiday; playing buses on the stairs (my parents had to pay to go up – "Hold very tight please, ding ding!"); playing nuns (I used to turn my bedroom into an imaginary dormitory, such as we had at boarding school, and my mother was always wonderfully participatory – "How are the children today, Sister?"); gathering bluebells, lilies-of-the-valley and lilacs from the little back garden to take to school for the May time procession; playing "bandicoots" and other animals with my mother; boxing matches with my dog, Benji; cockling in Poole Harbour and being on the beach at Sandbanks. At such times there was stillness; there was great absorption – and love.

I remember, as a child of about three, resolving to do better than the adults around me, whom I perceived as dishonest, complicated and unhappy. I saw the pain in people very clearly – such as the occasion of a cocktail party at my aunt's house during a weekend away from school. One of the guests was an old man. He had suffered a stroke and had previously been something of a drinker. He was in a wheelchair and on the tray in front of him was a glass of milk. From time to time someone would come up to him and slip some gin into it. He was maudlin, dribbling and pretty near incomprehensible.

I watched in horror from the other side of the room, until I could stand it no longer. I rushed out of the room and took refuge in one of the downstairs bedrooms. My aunt followed, to find me sobbing uncontrollably, gasping that I couldn't bear the brutality of what they were doing to that poor man. The deadness, hypocrisy and masked violence of that whole society sickened me. My aunt simply couldn't understand what was getting to me and I was told to "pull myself together" and rejoin the party.

> **Situation:** Two women stand on a country pathway, talking to a man in a car outside a caravan park. A small child stands behind the women, saying, "Come on, oh come on, *come on*", incessantly and repetitively, whilst tugging at the back of one of the women's trousers. All three adults ignore the child.
>
> **Situation:** A woman drags a toddler round a supermarket, whilst pushing a baby in a pushchair. The toddler pulls on her hand, whining, "Mu-umm can I have one of them? … Oh, but Mum, I want some sweets." The woman ignores her, except to throw an occasional downward and backward glance to the child, snapping, "No" and "Shut up!"
>
> **Situation:** A man sits with a little boy outside a café. The child is inconsolable, having just been refused an ice-cream. After remonstrating a bit, the man changes his mind and orders an ice-cream for his son.

It is essential, if you are serious about educating your child towards a spiritual life, that you *communicate* the ground rules for such a life.[4] The first of these is: "*I, as an adult, am attempting to live a life of truth and love. This means being honest with myself and in my relationships and doing my best to give up unhappiness when I find it creeping into me. That means that the policy in this house is that moods are not taken for granted, nor left unchallenged or uninvestigated. Rather, discussion and communication take place in order to arrive at practical solutions to problems, so that bad feelings do not build up in ourselves or between us.*"

It is not wise to just let children 'do their own thing.' Children need respect and they need listening to, but they also need standards and right discipline. They do not benefit from being allowed to do their own thing when it involves making themselves and others

---

[4] Please see Resources on page 87.

miserable. Allow a child to 'do his own thing' and you breed a neurotic child. Children thrive when they know where they are, that they are respected and what the rules are.

Educating children in a life of the spirit is a vast task – it covers as diverse areas as what to eat, what time to go to bed, how to deal with disagreements with school friends and how to approach unfamiliar animals – to name but a smattering of randomly chosen areas. I am not an expert and I am not attempting to cover this field exhaustively. What I am offering are pointers: key points gleaned from my experience of myself and my own childhood, and from years of observation of children. What I am aiming to do in making these points is to set the exercises in this book into the wider context of a child's total upbringing. A child is naturally meditative, as I have said, so the main work is *preventative* – that is working to stop his or her natural clarity, honesty, loving nature and true innocence from getting distorted or smothered.

Years ago, a friend, whenever her toddler decided to have a crying fit, would get down to his level, look him straight in the eyes and ask, "Why are you crying?" If the child offered a reason which had a practical and possible solution, she would act to remedy the source of the child's distress, explaining what she was doing in the process. If he could not give a reason, or merely wished to continue whimpering, without making any attempt to stop – she would firmly ask him to stop; pointing out the foolishness of weeping for no reason, or refusing to do something about the cause. This way of dealing with her tiny son was inspired by her own meditation practice. You may be tempted to say, "Ah, poor thing, he's only a child. He can't help it." Not true. If he's old enough to have a tantrum, he's old enough to learn how to stop a tantrum.

Once you see what a tantrum disguises, what it really *is* and what seeds of damaged unchallenged tantrums and moodiness sow for the future, it becomes a matter of urgency to help a child not to get into this state in the first place.

What is a tantrum? It is a dishonest emotional demand which attempts to manipulate and coerce others into getting what it wants. It is an unreasonable and exaggerated response of grief and rage to loss and disappointment. Indulge a tantrum in a child and you sow the seeds of a discontented adult. A sullen boy grows into a morose, resentful, uncommunicative man. A hysterical girl grows into a nagging, dissatisfied woman.

Obviously, it goes without saying; that the adult needs to be doing all this first. If not, it would have little meaning to pass it on to the child. Much of what I am criticizing here passes today as completely normal. Because it is regarded as so normal to expect moodiness and disruptive behaviour in children, it takes courage at first as a parent to start to deal with the problem, but the rewards are well worth the effort.

What are the key points here?

Respecting the child as an intelligent being.
Communicating with the child.
Considering and taking the child's experience seriously.

Helping the child to distinguish real distress (such as having grazed a knee) from emotional demand (such as having been asked politely and kindly to stop interrupting a conversation between two adults).

Encouraging the child always to look for the cause of a problem and to take immediate practical action to dissolve it.

Another key point is to keep the child's attention *in the present moment*. For example, a bump on the head is a real shock, but we have all seen how the unhappiness already resident in the child can attach itself to such a situation to milk it for more than it was originally worth. This needs to be pointed out. Such shocks respond well to a gentle hand, a soft voice, a kiss and 'Rescue Remedy'.

Another key point is not to let patterns of avoidance or impertinence build up. This may mean not taking "no" or "don't know" for an answer when there's a mood or sulk about. Just as an adult in living the life of the spirit needs to be ever vigilant within himself, so does he need to be in the face of hereditary unhappiness he sees reflected back to him in the child.

"What is *really* going on?" can be a useful question. "You're obviously being rude, sullen, offhand, dismissive, aggressive, etc. because something is troubling you, because when you're happy you don't behave like that – so *what* is going on? What's the problem? The sooner we can get it out and talk about it, the quicker we can solve it."

Overload, Rest and Processing

Children, from a younger and younger age are suffering from a plethora of input. High levels of stimuli, speed and noise assault them at school, at home and at play. This excess has the effect of lessening a child's contact with his or her inner reality – eventually, in many cases, dissolving it completely. How many men do you know who have difficulty identifying or expressing what they feel? How many women do you know who deny, push down or violate their feelings and needs?

The language of '*should, must* and *ought to*' is the language of self-violation, and its grammar is learned very young. "I should be able to cope with this... Ought to be more interested in this... I must keep going... When my body is screaming for rest, screaming for peace, screaming for something honest and natural."

If you bombard a child loudly enough and for long enough, eventually he will no longer be able to hear himself and he will start to identify himself as, and value himself in terms of, what he perceives externally – how others are and how he thinks they want him to be. He will become unresponsive (though he may be reactive), irresponsible and manipulable. His innate intelligence will cease to shine and he will no longer be truly creative – in the sense of original and at one with the source of wisdom and inspiration in himself. This is now a relentless and inevitable process in our civilized schooling machine. The solution lies with the intelligence and responsibility of the individual adult.

Time to digest, absorb, integrate and rest is essential in a growing child's life and this needs to be built into a daily routine, such as resting in a darkened room for 20 minutes after school, or a short period of meditation before leaving for school, before meals and before bed at night. Periods of reflection, assessment and discussion are important. Conscious gaps introduced to punctuate the busyness of the day are useful; consciously using the time between things to be still.

Many children I see are in panic and turmoil inside. They are scrambled by the sheer speed and complexity of the environment in which they are having to live their lives. Healers I know have confirmed the same findings to me in their endeavour to unravel the results of this scrambling; manifesting as the symptoms of eczema, digestive problems and other illnesses.

Taking Care of Yourself

You need to be taking care of your own needs to deal fully with the real needs of your child. Anything you cannot cope with in your child is something that is unconscious in you, or that you have not mastered in yourself. Children reflect the lack of self-discipline of their parents (or the adults in their environment). I am not trying to pretend that any of this is easy. I know it takes great courage, determination and staying power, but it *is* possible.

You have to put your own real needs first, which means giving up your enslavement to oughts and shoulds and what everyone else tells you is the right way to be doing it, as well as to some of your conditioned (self-destructive) preferences. If you're wrecked, you are no good to anyone. We take so much for granted, we are so used to exhausted mothers and hyped-up children that we think it is normal. The adults to whom I have taught meditation have often been relieved to learn that they do not need to be tyrannized by their children!

Children's Questions

"Do cows think?"
"Have trees got feelings?"

My mother was great with questions. She realized that, if I was old enough to ask a question, I was old enough to know the answer. I never got a "shut up" or "you're too young to know about such things" from her in response to any of my genuine questions. This was one of her greatest gifts to me, for in it she demonstrated her love and respect for me, and fostered a lifelong enthusiasm for learning, and the spirit of fearless enquiry.

Sometimes I asked embarrassing questions at the wrong time and in the wrong place. On such occasions, looking very secretive, she would bend down, her finger to her lips and whisper, "I'll tell you later." She always kept her word.

On one occasion, I must have been about ten, she was cleaning the bath and I was standing at the wash basin.

"Mummy...?" I asked.

"Yes darling."

"Father Christmas doesn't really exist, does he?"

"What do you mean?"

"It's Daddy, isn't it?"

"Well, yes darling, it is."

As simple as that.

She never patronized me. A cow was a cow from day one – never a "moo-moo". There were many moments of precious and intimate communication which were sparked off by my innocent questions. My mother always answered me clearly and honestly – tailoring her responses to my level of understanding, and she always had the courage to say "I don't know."

I learned from both my parents that more pain is caused by shilly-shallying and pussy-footing around sensitive issues or ones which are conventionally considered to be embarrassing than by coming straight out with it and calmly and maturely calling a spade a spade. I have referred here to conversations with my *mother*, because, being female, it was to my mother that I turned for answers to knotty or intimate questions. Fathers, of course, play as crucial a role in bringing up male children, who rely on them for the reflection of informed and honest masculinity.

Meditation in Schools

The purpose of meditation is to access stillness, awareness and self-knowledge. Some of the side-effects of a regular meditation practice which are of particular relevance in a school are increased clarity, ability to pay attention and to focus, efficiency and improved memory. Stillness saves energy that is wasted in fiddling, fidgeting, day-dreaming, fantasy and excess talking, as well as putting more energy into doing things than is necessary.

One way of integrating the exercises in this book is to break up the school day into separate units and to use particular exercises at particular times.

Here are Some Suggestions:

1. Before School:
Making friends with my body (massage).

Sitting in silence.

Smiling Sun Flower.

2. During Lessons:
One thing at a time.

Breathing out to relax and release thought and tension.

Stillness to access information.

Paying attention to the *way* we do things.

Writing/painting after meditation.

One-minute 'breather' – Pin-Drop Exercise.

Ssh! What Can you Hear? Exercise.

Describing experiences to a neighbour and/or class.

Inside/Outside Exercise when interacting with others.

3. Between Lessons:

Being in body between activities, going to the toilet etc.

Watching breathing.

Anchoring in feet.

Stretching-Growing Exercise.

4. At Lunch:

Not talking while eating.

Magic Meal Exercise.

Responsibility for moods (self-observation).

Breathing the Sky Exercise.

5. After School:

Consciously close the day with short rituals, for example:

- Review what you've learned today (including about yourself), what you enjoyed and what you are grateful for.
- Healing breathing – radiate benefits to others.
- Wise Being Exercise before going home.

Note for Parents and Teachers:

We can only transmit to children what we have practised and what we know and are ourselves. I would suggest, therefore, that before you try any of this book with a child, you familiarize yourself with the exercises, perhaps practising each one daily for a week before moving on. This will be particularly useful if you have not meditated before.

You might find it helpful to record the exercises, reading them slowly to give yourself plenty of time to carry out and fully experience each step, and then play them back to yourself. This will also help to make you more sensitive to pace, tone and timing whilst doing them with the children.

I would suggest to parents, teachers and friends that you choose specific regular times for building up a connection with the exercises – such as last thing at night, before class, between lessons, at meal times, in the car, in the bath, and so on.

It is important that you don't proceed until the child has mastered sitting absolutely still and the Smiling Sun Flower exercise. Once you know the exercises well, you may find that you can adapt and develop them to suit the circumstances.

Making friends with my body

(Introductory Physical Exercises)

Purpose/Focus
a. To deepen awareness of the body.
b. To align body and mind.
c. To encourage pleasure in embodiment.

A. WARMING UP

STAND STILL AND CLOSE YOUR EYES.

Feel the weight of your body balanced evenly on your feet.

Feel as though the top of your head is looking at the ceiling.

NOW GENTLY EXPLORE INSIDE YOUR BODY TO SEE IF THERE ARE ANY TIGHT PLACES:

...the eyes...?...the forehead...?...the jaw...?...the shoulders...?

...the hands...?...the chest...?...the tummy...?...the legs...?

...the bottom...?...the knees...?...the feet...?

LET YOUR BREATH COME AND GO NATURALLY

AND FEEL THAT IT'S VERY SOFT AND GENTLE.

LET YOUR LIPS REST LIGHTLY TOGETHER,

OR LET YOUR MOUTH BE SLIGHTLY OPEN.

SEE IF YOU CAN MELT ANY TIGHT PLACES

WITH YOUR GENTLE BREATH.

Even the roots of your hair and your teeth can relax.

NOW START TO RUB YOUR HANDS TOGETHER.

FEEL THE TEXTURE OF YOUR SKIN, AND LISTEN TO THE SOUNDS YOUR HANDS MAKE... NOW RUB YOUR HANDS TOGETHER FASTER...

DO YOU FEEL ANY HEAT? WHERE DO YOU FEEL IT?

NOW, USING YOUR LOVELY WARM HANDS, GENTLY RUB YOURSELF ALL OVER YOUR BODY. SOME PLACES, LIKE THE BACK AND LEGS, YOU MAY FIND YOU WANT TO RUB MORE VIGOROUSLY.

LET THE WARM GLOW FROM YOUR HANDS SPREAD INTO

AND AROUND EVERY TINY CELL OF YOUR BODY.

WHEN YOU'RE READY, OPEN YOUR EYES

AND COME BACK TO THE ROOM.

Teacher's Note:
In the next exercise I suggest using music. This is the only exercise in the book to which this applies. I would discourage you from using music or poetry, or any other relaxation 'device' or mood enhancer. The purpose of meditation is to cultivate stillness and clarity. Part of its function is to wean us from associative imagery and other external props.

B. GROWING STRAIGHT

(This could be accompanied by music or atmospheric sounds)

STAND STILL & RELAXED, AND CLOSE YOUR EYES.

GO THROUGH THE BODY IN THE WAY YOU LEARNT IN (A).

NOW CURL UP VERY SMALL ON THE FLOOR.

STAY RELAXED, AND KEEP YOUR EYES CLOSED.

IMAGINE YOU'RE IN A LARGE AND BEAUTIFUL SPRING MEADOW.

(The outside landscape can be varied from garden to wilderness at the discretion of the guide) –

All around, the soft green grass stretches for miles, and the sound of the birds and the perfumes of many wild flowers are all around you.

WHAT FLOWERS CAN YOU SMELL?

You are a tiny seed resting in the earth... Waiting for the time to grow. As you rest, a light shower of rain begins to fall... It soaks into you and you hungrily, gratefully, drink it up... As you do, you feel your roots beginning to grow out of the bottoms of your feet, and begin to burrow their way down into the damp, crumbly earth. You feel yourself getting a little bigger and

S--T--R--E--T--C--H--I--N--G.

As you begin to E...X...P...A...N...D you feel the lovely old Sun filtering down on your back, as the rain clouds disappear. The Sun grows warmer, and warmer, and warmer and, as it shines, you RISE to meet the radiant heat...

SLOWLY s-t-r-e-t-c-h-i-n-g.

R-e-a-c-h-i-n-g......g-r-o-W-I-N-G.

UP...and...OUT...and...UP...and...OUT.

Until you are as TALL and as OPEN as you can be.

FEEL THE ROOTS GROWING OUT OF THE SOLES OF YOUR FEET, ANCHORING YOU INTO THE RICH, BROWN EARTH.

FEEL YOUR LEAVES WAVING IN THE WIND.

What sort of a plant are you?

TURN YOUR FACE TO THE SUN AND LET A SMALL

SMILE COME ONTO YOUR LIPS,

As you drink up its warmth.

What can you feel, smell, hear... All around you?

How has the meadow changed since you were a small seed?

And now...

YOU CAN OPEN YOUR EYES AND SLOWLY LOOK AROUND.

BEFORE YOU START

The best way to work through this book is SLOWLY.

Give yourself plenty of time for each exercise and do each one several times until it comes easily, before you move on to the next one.

BEFORE YOU START –

PRACTICE SITTING ABSOLUTELY STILL FOR ONE MINUTE.

DON'T MOVE AT ALL – NOT EVEN A TINY BIT OF YOU,

BUT DON'T HOLD YOUR BREATH.

ONLY START THE EXERCISES WHEN YOU CAN SIT COMPLETELY STILL

FOR AT LEAST ONE MINUTE.

Teacher's Note:

You might try starting with "hearing a pin drop" as a way of getting into this, and then progressing to "hearing the feather drop." It might even be useful occasionally to start with "hearing the frying pan drop!"

It may also be useful to choose some form of signal – such as the 'ting' of an oriental-style bell/cymbal – to indicate that a meditation session is about to commence. Or a variety of different sounds could be used to indicate different things, e.g. wooden spoon, maracas, bell, or 'ting' – sit down; 'ting, ting' – silence; 'ting, ting, ting' – close your eyes and listen. N.B. Stillness is essential. Without stillness, we can't stop thinking and without absence of thought, we cannot begin to enter into real meditation.

Smiling Sun Flower

1

Purpose/Focus
a. To harmonize breath, body and awareness.
b. To emphasize basic goodness.

Teacher's Note:
Read slowly, leaving plenty of space between each instruction.

SIT DOWN AND CLOSE YOUR EYES.

How do you feel?

LET YOUR BACK BE STRAIGHT, BUT NOT STIFF.
BE VERY STILL.
LET YOURSELF FEEL THAT YOU'RE SETTLING INTO A WARM BATH.

Is your jaw relaxed? Behind the eyes...?

CHECK YOUR SHOULDERS AND BOTTOM ARE RELAXED.

It will be easier if at first you –

BREATHE OUT, AS IF YOU WERE SIGHING

Haaaaaaaa... very softly...

KEEP THE BACK OF YOUR THROAT OPEN, SOFT AND YIELDING.
LET ANY TIGHTNESS YOU FEEL MELT AWAY IN THE OUTBREATH.
NOW LET THE BREATH CHANGE TO...

Aaaaaaaaaah...

FEEL THE BREATHING FULL AND WARM
AND DEEP DOWN IN YOUR TUMMY.

**(Once the breath is relaxed, you can close your mouth and
continue to breathe naturally)**

SMILE GENTLY –

NOW, **keeping your eyes closed,**

FEEL YOURSELF OPEN… LIKE A FLOWER IN THE SUN.

FEEL THE WARMTH ON YOUR FACE

AND IN YOUR TUMMY…

LET IT SPREAD DOWN YOUR LEGS,

AND UP INTO YOUR HEART…

AND DOWN YOUR ARMS…

LET ALL PICTURES AND THOUGHTS DISSOLVE AS THEY COME

JUST REST WITHIN THIS WARM, OPEN, SMILING FEELING

NOW… STILL BREATHING SOFTLY –

GENTLY OPEN YOUR EYES… AND LOOK AROUND.

**(This can be practised for one or two minutes at a time.
You can sit for longer once you know the exercise)**

2 Ssh! What Can You Hear?

Purpose/Focus
a. To encourage investigation of a sense other than sight.
b. To develop simultaneous concentration and relaxation.
c. To experience direct perception (without categorisation/judgement).
d. To distinguish between response and reaction.

When you are outside in the garden, or walking in the country or park:

SIT DOWN, CLOSE YOUR EYES, AND… LISTEN.

What can you hear?

WHISPER QUIETLY EVERY NEW SOUND THAT YOU HEAR.

NOW, SILENTLY, CONCENTRATE ONLY ON THE SONGS

THE BIRDS ARE SINGING.

Don't reach out to listen to them, and don't name them in your mind.

JUST LET THE SOUNDS COME INTO YOU… AND PASS THROUGH YOU.

Can you let the sounds blend with your soft breath?

Remember not to screw yourself up into a knot.

Don't forget the Aaaaaaaaaaaaaaaahhh…

If you find yourself thinking or noticing anything else,

STOP, AND START ONLY NOTICING THE SOUNDS.

Can you hear the sound without telling yourself what's making it?

AND NOW… YOU CAN OPEN YOUR EYES AND LOOK AROUND YOU.

Additional Activities

◆ Recording different everyday sounds.

◆ Projects on regional accents and how voices distinguish people.

◆ Study of animal sounds.

◆ Writing about hearing and listening.

◆ Discussion: What is thought?

◆ Experiencing effects of different sounds and music.

3 When I Walk, I Just Walk – and When I Sit, I Don't Wobble!

Purpose/Focus

a. To bring body and mind into harmony.

b. To encourage 'grounding'.

c. To deepen stillness in movement.

d. To extend awareness of present time.

Once, a wise being in Japan said, "When sitting, just sit – don't wobble!" He meant that it is a good idea to do things with all of you. When you do things, not leaving any part of you out – not holding back, or thinking about something else – you do them well.

TRY WALKING FROM ONE END OF YOUR ROOM TO ANOTHER, QUITE SLOWLY…
IN A RELAXED WAY… **Letting your arms hang gently, loosely.** WITHOUT THINKING…
JUST WALKING… FEELING THE FEELINGS OF WALKING IN YOUR FEET…
IN YOUR LEGS… IN YOUR HIPS… IN YOUR CHEST… IN YOUR NECK… IN YOUR HEAD…
IN YOUR SHOULDERS… IN YOUR ARMS… IN YOUR HANDS…

Sometimes, when you're walking down the street – just say to yourself quietly:

"JUST WALKING… BODY JUST WALKING."

And let yourself

'FEEL WALKING WALKING' – WITHOUT ANY EFFORT ON YOUR PART –
WITHOUT ANY DISTRACTION.

Doing this will help you to do other things that you do with all of you – not leaving any part of you behind or to one side.

Additional Activities

◆ Try this "when I am walking, I just walk" idea with other things. For example, "when I am talking to a friend, I just talk to a friend." "When I am washing, I just wash." "When I am writing, I just write." Notice how your body knows what to do, without you having to make any effort.

◆ Get together with a small group and talk about the difference between how you individually feel when **all of you** is involved in something and when you leave bits of you out, or when you are distracted.

4 Breathing the Sky

Purpose/Focus

a. To encourage interest in colour and its relationship to mood and emotion.

b. To develop a quality of spaciousness and openness in which opportunities can arise, and understanding can grow.

c. To develop perspective.

Have you noticed that you can breathe in colours?

Try it, when you see a colour you like.

You can do this at home, at school, out shopping – anywhere, in fact.

It's especially good to do in the countryside or in a park.

When you look at the grass,

IMAGINE YOURSELF BREATHING IN ITS GREEN-NESS,

THE SKY – ITS BLUENESS,

A FLOWER – ITS YELLOWNESS, OR PINKNESS...

How do the different colours make you feel?

When you're outside on a bright day, see if you can –

BREATHE IN THE SKY, AND LET IT GO

AND BREATHE IT IN,

AND FEEL THE LIGHTNESS OF THE SPACE YOU ARE

AND HOW MUCH SPACE

IS ALL AROUND

AND... LET IT GO... AND...

Additional Activities

◆ Matching colours to emotions.

◆ What things are what colour and why (jewels, flowers, food)?

◆ What colours do you like wearing?

◆ What colours do you avoid? Why?

◆ Sharing experiences of Sky-Breathing.

◆ Find books, poems and stories about colour.

5 "I Don't Know" is a Good Place to Be

Purpose/Focus
a. To cultivate an empty, open, receptive state of being; capable of evolution.
b. To encourage the spirit of enquiry.
c. To foster access to real wisdom and useful knowledge, rather than mere information.

If you know about Jesus, you may know that he is supposed to have said: "Let the little children come to me, for theirs is the Kingdom of Heaven." That was an occasion when he was out with his friends, teaching lots of people and all the kids, because they really liked him, came running up to him. The grown-ups were trying to keep the kids away from Jesus, so they wouldn't bother him, but he said, "No, let them come to me." And on another occasion, he said "Unless you become as a little child, you cannot enter into the Kingdom of Heaven."

There was also more recently, certainly in my lifetime, a wise man who grew up in the country of Korea, and he used to say, "Only go straight. Only keep **don't know mind.**"*

Now I'd like you to take a few minutes, maybe split up into small groups, or discuss with your teacher, to **TALK ABOUT WHAT YOU THINK HE MIGHT HAVE MEANT BY "ONLY KEEP DON'T KNOW MIND."**

We're told so often these days about how important it is to know things and to know about things and to always have the answer to questions, and never to be in a state where you know less than the people around you, and so on. But, you know, it's not always such a bad thing not to know things, because when you don't know, your mind is open and ready to let new ideas, new knowledge, come in. But if you already know everything, there's no space for anything new, and pretty soon your mind becomes dull and stagnant.

* Korean Zen Master, Soen Sa Nim. You might also be interested in Suzuki Roshi's **Zen Mind, Beginner's Mind**.

When you consider those words:

ONLY GO STRAIGHT

and

ONLY KEEP DON'T KNOW MIND

and the name of the other exercise in this book called

WHEN I'M WALKING, I JUST WALK, AND WHEN I'M SITTING, I DON'T WOBBLE,

you might be able to see that there's a connection between these.

SEE IF YOU CAN FIND OUT,

when you are doing your walking and when you are keeping your mind open and "don't know" – if you can

DISCOVER WHAT THE CONNECTION IS BETWEEN THEM.

Additional Activities

◆ When you're faced with a challenge, or something new to do, which you feel might be difficult... **JUST RELAX... BREATHE OUT AND LET YOUR BODY AND BREATH SOFTEN... LET YOUR MIND BECOME VERY STILL AND EMPTY.** In that state, you will be ready to allow what you already know (which you may not know you already know) to come to the surface. You will also find good questions to ask and you will know who to ask, because a very important part of learning is knowing when to ask what questions and who to ask. Quite often, when we are faced with a new challenge, we tend to tighten up our bodies and our minds fill with thoughts. Both of these things make it much more difficult for us to approach the problem or the challenge or the situation in a way that will actually be useful to us.

◆ Can you begin to get an idea from this, how being still and being able to enter your inner silence helps you to be more creative and more efficient?

Saving Energy in my 'Piggy Bank' Inside

Purpose/Focus
a. To cultivate an awareness of personal energy.
b. To develop understanding of the symbiosis of planet and human.
c. To stimulate responsible Earth-stewardship.

There is a lot of talk these days about the energy crisis upon the Earth; about how the fossil fuels have nearly run out; about how we are destroying the rainforests; about how much waste and pollution we are making; about our unhealthy diet and about how many new diseases are being discovered.

But the energy crisis on the planet begins inside each of us. What's happening on the planet outside reflects what is going on in the people on the planet, inside. We are supposed to be looking after this planet. It is our home and our garden, and you don't drop rubbish all over the floor of your home, do you? Or at least if you do, you pick it up quickly.

In this exercise, I want to look at **THE WAYS WE ARE WASTING OUR ENERGY INSIDE US**, because if we can learn to stop wasting energy inside us, we will stop wasting energy outside as well.

WHAT ARE SOME OF THE WAYS THAT YOU CAN WASTE (OR HURT) THE ENERGY INSIDE YOURSELF?

You can do it by:

THINKING WHEN YOU DON'T NEED TO THINK, TALKING TOO MUCH, FIDGETING, TAPPING YOUR FEET ON THE FLOOR, CHEWING GUM, THROWING YOUR ARMS AND LEGS ABOUT AS YOU WALK.

See if you can think of other ways in which you waste energy in your life and

NOTICE WAYS IN WHICH GROWN-UPS AROUND YOU AND FRIENDS OF YOURS WASTE THEIR ENERGY.

You don't need to tell them about it. It is not a competition and it is not about judging people.

JUST WATCH AND SEE WHAT YOU SEE.

If you watch an animal – a cat washing itself, for instance – the cat will use just enough energy to do the job efficiently. The cat doesn't need to show off. It doesn't need to try to get attention. It just does what it needs to do; quietly and without fuss.

IF WE CAN LEARN TO DO THE THINGS THAT WE DO WITH THE GRACE AND DIGNITY OF A WASHING CAT, WE WILL SAVE A LOT OF ENERGY.

Here's a little exercise to help remind us of that:

SIT VERY STILL,

with a straight back, but relaxed.

IMAGINE INSIDE **(deep in your tummy)**, A PIGGY BANK...

It can look like a 'piggy' or it can just be a pot that the light shines through – it could be a glass pot; sitting deep in your tummy.

WHEN YOU BREATHE IN, IMAGINE THAT THE POT IS FILLING WITH ENERGY. EVERY TIME YOU BREATHE OUT, SEE THAT ENERGY RADIATING THROUGH THE TRANSPARENT WALLS OF THE CONTAINER, FILLING UP EVERY CELL IN YOUR BODY AND MAKING THEM GLOW.

As you breathe in – the energy is gathered. As you breathe out – the energy spreads to nourish your body. So,

WITH YOUR BREATH, YOU SAVE AND YOU CULTIVATE AND YOU MAKE YOUR ENERGY GROW...

This is a good exercise to do if you are feeling restless, instead of talking or rushing about.

Additional Activities

◆ Write down three ways by which you can save some energy in your life today.

◆ Talk to your family about ways that you can save energy at home.

◆ Look at the amount of rubbish that your family produces in one week and see if there are ways that you can use some of those things again; see if you can recycle more things and see if you can cut down on your rubbish. Every bit of rubbish that we produce has to go somewhere. It doesn't just vanish when it leaves the house. It has to be absorbed back into the earth, or the air or the water. And, if it is poisonous or harmful, it will damage them.

◆ What are the kinds of things that human beings do that pollute them **inside**? What can we do to reduce 'toxic waste' within ourselves?

(7) Stop-Start-Just a Minute...

a. To maintain inner stillness in the midst of activity.

b. To develop flexibility.

c. To nurture balance between 'field and content'.

When you come to the end of one activity and are just about to start another,

STOP FOR JUST A MINUTE.

STAND STILL, OR SIT DOWN,

CLOSE YOUR EYES AND LET YOURSELF BECOME VERY STILL.

BREATHE OUT, WITH AN OPEN SIGH... **Haaaaaah...**

AND LET GO OF EVERYTHING THAT YOU ARE HOLDING ONTO FROM WHAT YOU HAVE JUST DONE: **tension in the body, thoughts and pictures in the mind... Ideas about what you are going to do next...**

NOW YOU CAN MOVE INTO THE NEXT ACTIVITY, NEW AND REFRESHED.

This can be done in the middle of an activity, for instance, during a lesson, during a conversation, while playing outside or during a meal (YOU CAN THINK OF OTHER TIMES WHEN YOU COULD DO THIS).

STOP WHAT YOU'RE DOING...JUST STOP IN THE MIDDLE OF A SENTENCE, IN THE MIDDLE OF RUNNING, IN THE MIDDLE OF EATING...IN THE MIDDLE OF ANYTHING AND... BREATHE. NOTICE HOW STILL IT IS INSIDE YOURSELF... BREATHE OUT TENSION, BREATHE OUT HURRY, BREATHE OUT THINKING...

AND THEN... START AGAIN... AND THEN... STOP... BREATHE... START AGAIN... STOP...

Additional Activities

◆ Talk in class with your teacher and in small groups with your friends about how this exercise feels to you.

◆ Do you notice any difference in your day when you do this often?

◆ Can you feel the quietness inside when you're in the middle of doing something or talking?

◆ Write about doing this exercise during an activity at home, and at school.

(8) Breathe it Better

Purpose/Focus
a. To demonstrate how breathing can be used for healing.
b. To encourage using the mind creatively to heal.

When I was little, if I grazed my knee or accidentally hurt myself, my mother would always say, "Kiss it better," while she cuddled me and kissed the area that was hurt.

You can do the same for yourself, by using your breath to help you relax and get better.

IF YOU HAVE A SMALL ACCIDENT
OR A SHOCK OF ANY KIND,
SIT DOWN QUIETLY
AND PUT YOUR ATTENTION ON YOUR BREATHING.
BREATHE INTO THE AREA OF PAIN,
LET THERE BE A LOVING AND HEALING QUALITY IN YOUR BREATH AND BREATHE INTO THE PAIN.
BREATHE OUT THE PAIN, AND LET YOUR MUSCLES RELAX
WHEN YOU BREATHE OUT.

Sometimes, when we're in pain, or hurt, we tense up with the shock and this makes the pain worse and stops us getting better. If you breathe out like this and relax, you will feel better much more quickly and not add any extra trouble on top of what has already happened to you (of course, you may also need to wash your graze, put a plaster on your cut, or do whatever your parents or the doctor recommend).

You can also add a colour to your breath. This is something I do if I accidentally burn my arm when taking something out of a hot oven. It works very well, as well as cooling the arm down under cold water, of course. It is a bit like what we do in the Breathing the Sky exercise, but you can use it specially for healing yourself, and other people or animals.

GENTLY PLACE YOUR HANDS AROUND YOUR CUT

OR BUMP OR SORE PLACE.

RELAX AND BREATHE INTO IT, THEN BREATHE OUT THE PAIN.

NOW SEE A VERY LIGHT, PALE GREEN COLOUR FLOWING IN YOUR BREATH

(it's as though your breath has turned green)

AND MOVING ALL AROUND AND INSIDE THE PLACE WHERE YOU ARE SORE.

LET YOUR GREEN BREATH WORK ITS MAGIC IN YOU.

You can also do this with pale blue or a silvery colour. These colours will relax you and COOL YOU DOWN and balance you if you are upset.

ALSO EXPERIMENT WITH GOLDEN COLOURS, AND WITH WARM ORANGEY AND YELLOWEY ONES.

How do these feel? When do you think it would be a good time to use these?

Additional Activities

◆ What other kinds of healing are there?

◆ What else might help us get better, as well as or instead of taking medicines?

9 Feeling Friendly Again

Purpose/Focus

a. To discover the arbitrariness of emotion.

b. To experience emotion as flexible bodily energy, rather than as fixed thought.

c. To develop responsibility for one's condition.

Next time you feel fidgety, upset or unhappy (maybe you have had a quarrel with a friend or are in trouble at home or at school),

SIT DOWN QUIETLY BY YOURSELF

AND

PRACTISE SMILING SUN FLOWER

Don't let yourself get up until you feel friendly with yourself again, and until you can feel the warm feeling inside your tummy and even in your toes.

Sometimes when we feel bad, we need to do something about a problem in our life – maybe we need to talk it over with someone. At other times, we just feel bad and there's nothing to be done except let the bad feeling go.

This exercise is to help you to do that.

Additional Activities

◆ Act emotions and feel how they arise and where they go in the body.

◆ Is there anything good about our 'bad' feelings? What is hidden inside: anger, fear, sadness…? Can these feelings be helpful to us in any way?

Teacher's Note:
Encourage children to share feelings at certain times of the day: when something of significance occurs to one of them, encourage the others to listen with full attention.

10 The Mood Game

Purpose/Focus
a. To develop awareness of, and sensitivity to, others.
b. To introduce an understanding of inter-relationship.

Before starting all the games, settle quietly for a little while and find the warm Smiling-Sun-Flower-feeling inside yourself.

When you meet someone –
NOTICE WHAT SORT OF MOOD THEY SEEM TO BE IN.
Can you tell how they're feeling?
How?
How do YOU feel with this person?
WHERE DO YOU FEEL YOUR FEELINGS IN YOUR BODY?

Additional Activities

◆ Act different moods – how do they affect your breathing, posture, facial expression, gesture and movement?

◆ Mask-making of different moods.

(11) Abracadabra!*

Purpose/Focus
a. To encourage clarity of intention.
b. To train the focus of will for positive results.
c. To demonstrate responsibility and the connection between how we are, what happens to us and how we experience our world.

Your thoughts, your words and your actions are very powerful. By what you think, what you say and what you do, you create the world you experience; you attract to yourself people, events and situations which are in harmony with how you are yourself. This is why there is a saying, "Birds of a feather flock together."

This is an exercise in which we can learn how to create good things for ourselves and other people. We are going to use several powerful abilities we have built into us as humans, but sometimes no-one points them out to us or shows us how to use them.

In fact, everyone is using them all the time, but usually they do not realise they are.

These powerful abilities are:
IMAGINATION
VISUALISATION
ATTENTION
WILL

* There are several meanings attributed to the word Abracadabra! It is a cabalistic word intended to suggest infinity and it was used as a charm to cure toothache, fevers, etc. Some say it comes from Hebrew, and comprises nine letters. Often the syllables were arranged in a triangular formation for talismanic effect. Arranging the letters in a downward-pointing triangle, makes them act as a funnel to channel celestial energies.

PART ONE

CLOSE YOUR EYES.

TAKE THREE DEEP BREATHS, AND LET GO ON EACH OUTBREATH.

RELAX.

TAKE IN ANOTHER DEEP BREATH AND RAISE YOUR SHOULDERS UP AS FAR AS

YOU CAN, AS THOUGH YOU'RE TRYING TO COVER YOUR EARS.

HOLD YOUR BREATH A MOMENT.

NOW BREATHE OUT AND LET YOUR SHOULDERS DROP AS YOU LET GO OF

ANY TENSION THAT'S LEFT IN YOUR BODY.

I am going to ask you to imagine a series of things.

AS SOON AS YOU CAN SEE OR FEEL THEM, RAISE ONE OF YOUR HANDS

FOR A MOMENT, TO LET ME KNOW THAT YOU ARE WITH ME...

BUT KEEP YOUR EYES CLOSED ALL THE TIME WE ARE DOING THIS EXERCISE.

IMAGINE YOU ARE SITTING ON THE BEACH.

FEEL THE SAND UNDER YOUR HANDS AND THE WARMTH OF THE SUN SHINING ON YOUR FACE, AND A LITTLE GENTLE BREEZE RUFFLING YOUR HAIR.

HEAR THE SOUND OF THE WAVES ON THE SHORE, CHILDREN PLAYING NEARBY, DOGS BARKING IN THE DISTANCE, SEAGULLS CRYING OVERHEAD.

TASTE THE SALT FROM THE SEA IN THE WIND, AS YOU BREATHE IN.

SMELL THE SLIGHT SALTINESS IN THE AIR.

NOW, STILL KEEPING YOUR EYES CLOSED...

LOOK AROUND YOU AND **SEE** THE SEA, AND ALL THE THINGS ON THE BEACH.

OPEN YOUR EYES AND SIT QUIETLY FOR A MOMENT.

To do this exercise, you used the power of your imagination and your ability to visualise. You also focused your will and intention in order to do it at all.

It's a good idea to GET UP AND SHAKE before you start Part Two.

PART TWO

In Part One we used our imagination to remember something we already know — being on the beach.

In this part we are going to use imagination, visualisation, attention and will to create something we haven't got. What we actually do is draw this to us from somewhere else, because everything we need already exists somewhere.

Sometimes people say they can't visualise. Visualisation is only the part of imagination which involves **seeing** — it is seeing with your eyes closed, or seeing something with your mind's inner eye, while your eyes are open looking at something else.

Everybody can do it.

TRY IT NOW.

CLOSE YOUR EYES AND THINK OF AN ORANGE.

GOT IT?

THAT'S VISUALISATION…!

NOW OPEN YOUR EYES AND THINK OF A GREEN CAMEL

WHILE YOU ARE SEEING THE ROOM YOU ARE IN.

HOW DID THAT GO?

WRITE DOWN THREE THINGS YOU WOULD LIKE.

Think about this for a little while. It is important that you do this carefully and ask yourself:

1. Is this a good thing for me to have?
2. Will it harm me, or anyone else, to have it?

When you are sure it's a helpful thing and it won't hurt anyone for you to have it — add it to your list.

THEN CHOOSE ONE OF THE THINGS — the one that is the most important to you; that you want the most.

NOW CLOSE YOUR EYES.

SETTLE DOWN AND TAKE A FEW DEEP BREATHS AS YOU RELAX

AND CONCENTRATE LIGHTLY INSIDE.

IMAGINE A FINE CRYSTAL BALL FORMING BETWEEN THE PALMS OF YOUR HANDS.

It looks like a soap bubble, you can see through it, and it is very light.

LET THE CRYSTAL BALL GROW A LITTLE BIGGER

AND SIT WITHIN YOUR UPTURNED HANDS.

NOW IMAGINE THE THING YOU WANT IN THE MIDDLE OF THE CRYSTAL BALL,

SEE IT AND FEEL IT VERY CLEARLY. REALLY KNOW IT IS THERE.

ALSO NOTICE HOW YOU FEEL KNOWING THAT YOU NOW HAVE THAT THING.

Now we are going to send the crystal bubble off into the universe – to the place it needs to go, to allow the thing you want to create to appear in your life.

WATCH AS THE BUBBLE BEGINS TO FLOAT UPWARDS AWAY FROM YOUR HANDS, HIGHER AND HIGHER, TOWARDS THE CEILING, LIGHTLY FLOATING HIGHER

AND HIGHER, OUT OF THE BUILDING WHERE YOU ARE, OFF INTO THE SKY.

LET IT GO TO WHEREVER IT NEEDS TO GO… AND FORGET ABOUT IT…

All you have to do now is wait for what you want to come to you when the time is right for you and everyone else.

There are some rules to follow which help this exercise to work very well:

1. DO IT OFTEN **(early in the morning or before sleeping are good times).**

2. DON'T WORRY ABOUT HOW THE THING YOU WANT WILL COME TO YOU **(you may not have to buy it yourself, because someone may give it to you, and it may not come to you in a way that you would expect).**

3. GIVING AND RECEIVING WORK AS 'TWO SIDES OF A COIN' IN OUR LIVES. IF YOU ARE A GENEROUS AND KIND PERSON, YOU WILL FIND THAT OTHER PEOPLE ARE GENEROUS AND KIND WITH YOU.

4. BEHAVE AS THOUGH YOU ALREADY HAVE THE THING YOU WANT – BE HAPPY, BE GRATEFUL, IMAGINE HOW YOU WOULD FEEL – AND FEEL IT NOW!

NOW REPEAT THE CRYSTAL BUBBLE EXERCISE, BUT THIS TIME, IMAGINE SOMETHING THAT YOU KNOW ONE OF YOUR FAMILY OR FRIENDS REALLY NEEDS AND WANTS, AND SEND THE BUBBLE INTO THE UNIVERSE FOR THEM.

Additional Activities

◆ Discussion about prayer.

◆ Explore the meaning of Jesus' words, "It is in giving that we receive."

◆ Are there similar teachings in all the world's religions? What are they?

◆ Write about generosity and gratitude.

◆ Try giving away to others things you would like to receive. For instance, if you would like more presents, practise giving people presents.

12 Inside-Outside

Purpose/Focus

a. To maintain inner stability in disruptive situations.

b. To investigate the nature of distraction.

c. To develop a solid sense of inner calm.

d. To nurture mental flexibility.

When you're with someone else,

SEE IF YOU CAN STAY IN TOUCH WITH YOUR GOOD, WARM FEELING

INSIDE AT THE SAME TIME AS BEING WITH THE OTHER PERSON

(You don't need to let the other person know you're doing this).

Does it change the way you are with this person?

Does it make a difference to what happens or to how they are?

DO THIS WHEN YOU ARE:

PLAYING / WORKING / TALKING

Which is the easiest time?

Which is the most difficult?

How does it feel?

When you are friends with yourself, you can sometimes help other people to make friends with themselves, too. Have you noticed that when you are happy, other people also seem to be happy? Or, if they're not, it doesn't upset you. Often, just because you're feeling your Warm Sun Flower Feeling inside and all around you – other people start to cheer up too!

Additional Activities

◆ Do two things at once without becoming wild, tense or confused.

◆ Talk about the things that are distracting. Under what circumstances is it difficult to stay calm?

13 Animal and Plant Friends

a. To promote respect for all living creatures.

b. To give a chance for fears and prejudices about different creatures (like spiders, crocodiles and maggots!) to be aired and examined.

c. To encourage responsibility for the totality of our environment.

d. To develop subtle vision and harness the imagination to positive use.

Next time you stroke a cat, or any animal (maybe your favourite pet?),

FEEL THE LIFE IN THE ANIMAL.

Is this life the same as yours?

BE VERY GENTLE, VERY **STILL**, WITH THIS ANIMAL.

Maybe you'd like to speak softly or sing to this animal?

Plants also respond to kindness. Everything that is alive responds to kindness. Actually – even machines and things that aren't alive do too. Like us, plants grow strong and stay healthy if they are in a loving atmosphere. That means if the people around them are loving and if the place where they are feels happy.

IMAGINE THE INSIDE OF A LEAF… MAKE IT VERY BIG… WALK AROUND INSIDE IT… NOW COME OUT… AND SEE THE LEAF SMALL AGAIN.

What's it like on the inside of a leaf… A petal… A tree?

Additional Activities

◆ Discussions about life and death.

◆ Visits to animal rescue centres and vets.

◆ Plant experiments: different feeds, music, care.

◆ Experiments with how feelings affect inanimate things.

14 Magic Meal

Purpose/Focus
a. To focus on smell, taste and touch.
b. To bring awareness and gratitude to eating and nourishment.
c. To discover interdependency.

Teacher's Note: This exercise is to be done with a real meal and real food.

PAUSE FOR A MOMENT'S QUIET.

This helps you to let go of what you have just been doing and to let your tummy know that you are about to eat.

CLOSE YOUR EYES, TAKE A FEW, SLOW, GENTLE BREATHS AND RELAX YOUR BODY BEFORE YOU EAT.

Doing this helps you digest your food better. Do this with everybody holding hands around the table or just sitting quietly.

LOOK AT ALL THE DIFFERENT KINDS OF FOOD ON YOUR PLATE. CONSIDER FOR A MOMENT WHERE THEY'VE ALL COME FROM AND ALL THE DIFFERENT PEOPLE WHO HELPED TO BRING THEM TO YOUR PLATE.

Such as the farmer, the man who drove the truck to market, the woman behind the till at the supermarket checkout, and so on.

SEE HOW MANY PEOPLE YOU CAN THINK OF.

You could even include the men who worked in the factory where the cooker which cooked your meal was made...

Without the hard work and help of all these people,

we would not have anything to eat.

NOW EAT PART OF THE MEAL WITHOUT TALKING.

EAT SLOWLY, CHEW EVERY MOUTHFUL VERY WELL.

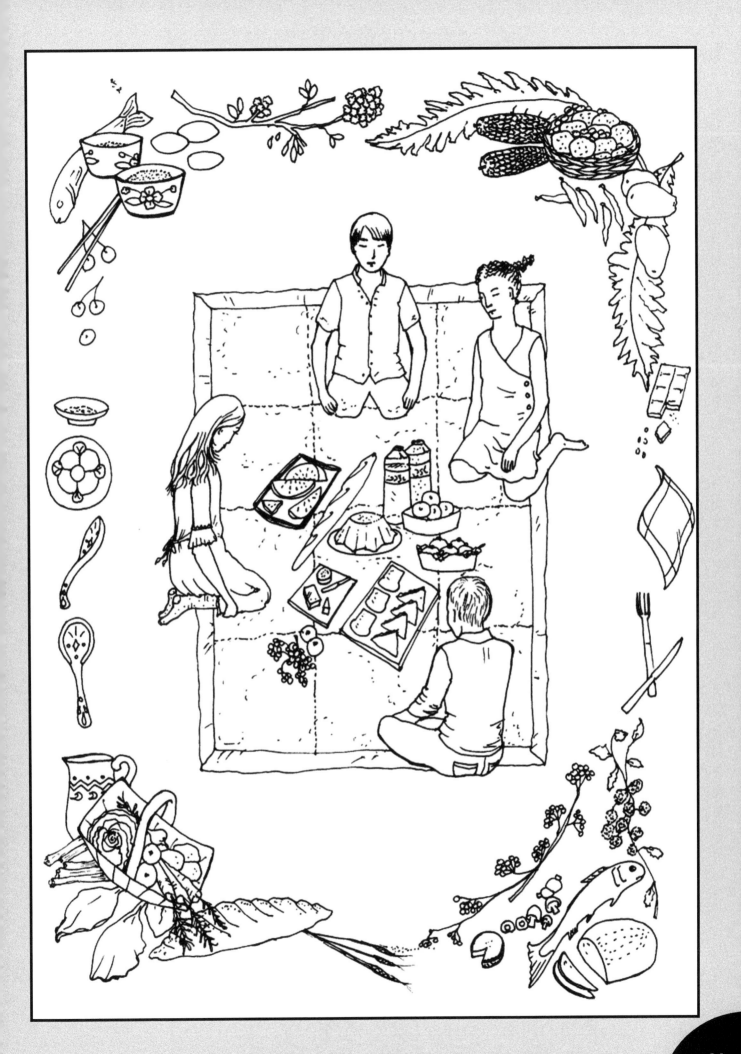

If you feel yourself getting fidgety or wanting to talk, you'll have to breathe deeply and relax inside a bit deeper before you continue. You may find it helps to close your eyes.

All the food you're eating started in the earth. You're eating the rain and the sunshine and the starlight...

SEE IF YOU CAN NOTICE THE DIFFERENCE BETWEEN SMELLING, TASTING AND FEELING THE FOOD. NOTICE WHAT YOUR TONGUE, TEETH AND LIPS ARE DOING.

Additional Activities

◆ Act out an imaginary meal with famous or mythical characters – what would they eat? How would they dress? What would they talk about?

◆ Project on food and colour.

◆ Project on nutritional food vs. junk food.

◆ Cooking styles in other countries.

◆ Keep a food diary and begin to notice how what you eat and drink affects you.

Earth, Water, Fire, Air and Space 15

Our planet, Earth, is made up of five **elements**, or basic parts: earth, water, fire, air and space.

> SEE IF YOU CAN BRING TO MIND WHERE YOU WOULD FIND
>
> THESE FIVE DIFFERENT ELEMENTS.
>
> YOU COULD COLLECT PICTURES OF DIFFERENT EXAMPLES.

Our bodies are also made up of these same five elements: bones and muscles are earthy parts of us; blood is watery; the fiery quality helps us digest our food and keeps us warm and air moves in and out of our lungs. Space separates, connects and contains everything.

> SEE IF YOU CAN DISCOVER PARTS OF THE BODY WHICH ARE MORE OF ONE ELEMENT THAN ANOTHER, OR WAYS IN WHICH THE ELEMENTS WORK WITHIN US.

Hidden inside these elements are qualities and we find these in our minds and characters. They have helpful and not-so-helpful faces, for instance:

If you are an earth person you may be patient, very even-tempered, generous, reliable and practical and able to see things in a balanced and fair way. On the other hand, you may be stubborn or proud and you may collect or hoard things – you may not like change.

If you are a water person you will probably be sensitive to the feelings of others, you may be quite flexible and adaptable or you may be poetic or imaginative. You may see things very clearly and be able to understand what is going on in other people or situations, perhaps quicker than other people do. On the other hand, you may be timid, or shy or fearful, you may find it difficult sticking to things and change your mind easily or you may be angry or irritable, like a churned-up pool or rushing waterfall.

If you are a fire person you will probably be warm-hearted and generous and caring about others. You could be very good at knowing the difference between things that are healthy and not so healthy (and not just for your body, but for the whole of you and other people). You may easily spot the difference between what is true and not true, just and unfair, and be able to spot tiny differences between people and situations. You will probably be good at making friends and inspiring people and helping them to feel at home. On the other hand, you may seem a bit overpowering to some people, or rather greedy – appearing to consume everything in your path, like a forest fire; or you flit from one interest or friendship to the next. You may also not be so good at making wise choices.

Airy people often have their fingers in many pies. They have good ideas and love communication of all kinds; particularly, talking to people. They are often very good at getting things done, or they can be quite difficult to pin down and may do so many things at once that they end up doing nothing properly or not finishing anything! They may seem a bit scatty and can be nervous and snappy. At their worst, they can be envious or jealous, or imagine that people have bad intentions towards them which they don't. If you are more of an airy sort of person, you might be quite clever.

If you are a space person you may be dreamy and focus more within yourself than outside. You will have the great gift of being able to see all sides of a situation and understand much more about yourself, other people and what is going on than most people ever do. On the other hand, because you are capable of understanding and sensing so much, you may, from time to time, feel overwhelmed or become confused and you may also tend to be lazy or sleepy!

Of course, none of us is just one of these types and you may see yourself in quite a few of them. We all have several of these qualities, but we usually have more of some of them than others.

- ◆ WHICH OF THESE QUALITIES CAN YOU SEE IN YOURSELF?
- ◆ ASK YOUR BEST FRIEND TO WRITE DOWN WHICH S/HE SEES IN YOU – AND COMPARE THIS WITH HOW YOU SEE YOURSELF.
- ◆ WHICH OF THESE QUALITIES DO YOU HAVE LEAST OF?
- ◆ WHAT COULD YOU DO TO ENCOURAGE MORE OF THAT QUALITY TO GROW IN YOURSELF?

Earth fills up space.

Water binds things and allows them to flow.

Fire separates things into their different parts and purifies them.

Air makes relationships between things and brings change.

Space contains and makes sense of everything.

START OBSERVING THE FIVE ELEMENTS WHERE YOU SEE THEM.

NOTICE HOW DIFFERENT THEY ARE.

NOTICE HOW THEY HELP YOU IN YOUR LIFE.

When you are drinking a glass of water on a hot day,

NOTICE THE COLDNESS OF THE WATER AGAINST THE HEAT OF YOUR BODY.

NOTICE THE FEELING OF LIQUID AS THE WATER GOES DOWN YOUR THROAT.

Walking in the breeze:

FEEL HOW THE AIR MOVES BETWEEN THINGS.

NOTICE HOW IT DISTURBS THINGS,

AND HOW IT ENLIVENS THINGS.

WAKE UP TO THE IMPORTANCE OF THE ELEMENTS ALL AROUND YOU, AND TO THE ACTIVITY OF THE ELEMENTS WITHIN YOU.

Additional Activities

◆ See if you can discover how the element earth shows itself in your body.

◆ The blood flowing through the body is one of the ways that the water element shows itself. See if you can find other kinds of water in your body.

◆ Do the same with fire, air and space.

◆ See if you can find anything which is not made up of these five elements (when you break it down into its smallest, finest parts).

◆ Imagine each of the elements as a being and paint a picture of one of them.

◆ If this being could speak, what would it/he/she say to you and to the world?

◆ Does this being have a song or make a sound?

Every Body Dies

Purpose/Focus
a. To dissolve the taboos around discussing death.
b. To encourage the contemplation of death.
c. To facilitate discussion about death.

When I was young, our cat, Dizzy, died. We buried his body in the garden and my father wrote a little poem which he painted on a piece of wood and put it on Dizzy's grave. The poem said:

"If his whiskers had been longer,
His life might not have been so short."

What this means is that if Dizzy had had longer whiskers, he might not have been able to get through the gap in the fence which he squeezed through. He ran out onto the road and was run over by a car. Cats judge the width of spaces using their whiskers.

When I was a bit older, my mother died. This was a very big shock for me – and very painful, because no one had ever told me anything sensible or true about death.

When I was a lot older, my father died. That was a much easier experience for me because, by then, I had discovered that death is a part of life and something we can learn to make friends with.

Have you ever seen a dead body?

Maybe you have had a favourite pet who died, or maybe you know a person who died?

Sometimes people are afraid of death and don't want to talk about it, but death is quite natural. Every thing and every body dies. That is the same as saying that everything and everybody comes to an end. Nothing lasts forever – except life itself. The more we can understand this and the more we can talk about it, the less we need to be afraid of it, and the more we can help other people who are sad or lonely.

Let's think about it for a moment. A table is usually made of wood and has four legs. For it to be made, a tree had to die. When the table has been used for several years, it begins to show the signs of age – marks from tea cups, pressure marks from people leaning heavily on their paper when they write, stains of sauce, maybe even a few cat claw marks! Eventually, the table will fall to pieces. It will get woodworm, or rot, or be broken up and burned.

The tree that the table came from might have lived hundreds of years, but eventually, its leaves would grow no more and it would begin to look dry and bare. In time maybe it would be struck by lightning, or just start to crumble as insects and fungi began to make their home in its trunk and branches.

> MAKE A LIST OF 'BODIES' –
>
> THREE ANIMAL, THREE VEGETABLE AND THREE MINERAL.
>
> **(Your teacher will explain what this means – don't forget that human bodies come under 'animal')**
>
> TALK ABOUT HOW EACH OF THESE 'BODIES' DIES –
>
> WHAT HAPPENS WHEN IT DIES?
>
> HOW DO YOU KNOW IT IS DYING?
>
> HOW DO YOU KNOW IT IS DEAD?
>
> IS THAT THE END OF IT, OR DOES IT APPEAR AGAIN?

Everybody dies. But the most important part of every body – the actual life in them, the part of you that recognises what is being read to you now – that part never dies.

> CAN YOU FEEL THAT YOU ARE NOT JUST YOUR BODY?

When you are doing the exercises in this book, you go into your body and feel and notice many things, but the part of you that is feeling and noticing them is not your body. It is your AWARENESS – life itself in you.

SIT DOWN AND CLOSE YOUR EYES.

Can you ever remember a time when you were dead?

COVER YOUR EARS WITH YOUR HANDS.

KEEP YOUR EYES CLOSED.

LISTEN INSIDE.

NOW OPEN YOUR EYES AND UNCOVER YOUR EARS.

IF YOU HAD FORGOTTEN EVERYTHING YOU KNOW,

AND IF YOUR BODY HAD DISAPPEARED,

WHAT WOULD BE LEFT?

You may not be able to answer this question in words, but

NOTICE WHAT YOU SENSE; NOTICE WHAT HAPPENS INSIDE YOU, WHEN YOU ARE ASKED THIS QUESTION.

It is something you can ask yourself every so often, maybe once a year, on your birthday.

Additional Activities

◆ Write a poem in praise of a person or animal you love who has died.

◆ Gather dead leaves and insects, bring them to class and talk about how they seem to you.

◆ If you have seen a dead body, what did it look like? Was it the same as the person when they were alive? How did you feel seeing the body?

Starry Mantle 17

Purpose/Focus
a. To encourage meditation at night.
b. To build inner/outer relationship.
c. To develop the senses creatively.

There is an old, old, story from Tibet. In fact, the story is so old that no-one can quite remember exactly when it happened. It is about a thief. This thief was the best thief in the whole country. He never did honest work, but went from place to place; robbing as he went.

One day, quite suddenly, he started to feel very unhappy and began to realise that his life was pretty meaningless and that he had hurt a lot of people. He decided it was time to change, but he didn't know how to.

In those days, long ago in Tibet, there were wise men and women called yogis, yoginis and lamas. You may have heard of llamas, spelt with two 'l's, but this is **lama** spelt with only one L. This word means 'teacher', but not any kind of teacher. A lama is a special teacher who can teach you to make friends with your self (even the bits you may not like very much). He or she can help you understand yourself, and encourage you to become the very best you can be. One of the main things that lamas do is teach people how to meditate.

So, here he was, this tired old thief, and he had heard tell of a wise old lama, many valleys away, on the far side of days of mountain travel.

After many days of hard travel and nights of uncertainty, cold and fear, he finally arrived at the lama's hermitage.

As he walked up to the entrance, he saw the old man brewing tea, welcoming him with a smile, as though he had been waiting for him all along. When they had drunk their tea, the famous thief began to tell the lama about his miserable life and how he would like to change and that he had heard tell that he could help him.

The lama looked at him with a steady look which was a mixture of very kind and very fierce and said, "Hmm, so, what are you good at?" This was a surprising question to the thief who didn't see what this had to do with his very serious request.

"Well," the thief replied, sheepishly, "I'm not good at anything."

"Don't be silly," responded the old lama, "everyone's good at something."

"Well," said the robber, "I'm good at stealing."

"Splendid!" beamed the lama, to the thief's utter amazement. "Now I am going in for the night, but I want you to stay out here all night, wrapped in these blankets," the lama announced, "and, as you do; sit quietly, gaze up into the sky and just steal all the light from the stars into yourself."

In Smiling Sun Flower, we breathed in the sunlight and we also practised 'Breathing the Sky' – remember? Well, this exercise is to be done at night. You can do it in your garden, in the country, in the park, sitting on your balcony, or even sitting on your bed, with the window open and looking out into the stars.

SIT QUIETLY IN THE WAY YOU KNOW HOW TO, CLOSE YOUR EYES…

SOFTEN AND RELAX WITH EVERY BREATH,

AND LISTEN TO THE SILENCE OF THE NIGHT.

ENJOY THE STILLNESS –

FEEL AS THOUGH YOU'RE DRINKING IT IN WITH YOUR BREATH.

OPEN YOUR EYES AND GAZE UP INTO THE SKY… LET YOUR GAZE REST VERY LIGHTLY AND WIDELY ON THE SKY… DON'T TRY TO SEE… DON'T COUNT THE STARS OR TRY TO NAME THEM… JUST LET SEEING SEE… AND HEARING HEAR… AND FEELING FEEL…

NOW, OPEN YOUR ARMS WIDE; REACHING UP AND OUT TO THE SKY AND ITS MILLIONS OF TWINKLING STARS AND PLANETS… FEEL THE CONNECTION BETWEEN YOU AND THEM… THROUGH YOUR BREATH AND YOUR OUTSTRETCHED ARMS.

NOW VERY SLOWLY BRING YOUR ARMS BACK IN TOWARDS YOUR BODY.

AS YOU DO THIS, IMAGINE AND FEEL THAT YOU ARE DRAWING THE WHOLE

NIGHT SKY AROUND YOU… A DEEP… DARK… VELVETY… STARRY MANTLE…

COVERED IN MILLIONS OF DIAMOND CHIPS OF LIGHT.

CLOSE YOUR EYES, LET YOUR HANDS REST IN YOUR LAP AND BEGIN TO ABSORB THE LIGHT FROM THE MANTLE INTO YOUR BODY, THROUGH THE PORES OF YOUR SKIN, THROUGH YOUR BREATH… FEEL THE LIGHT ENTERING YOUR BLOODSTREAM AND FLOWING INTO EVERY CELL OF YOUR BODY **(sit with this for a while)**.

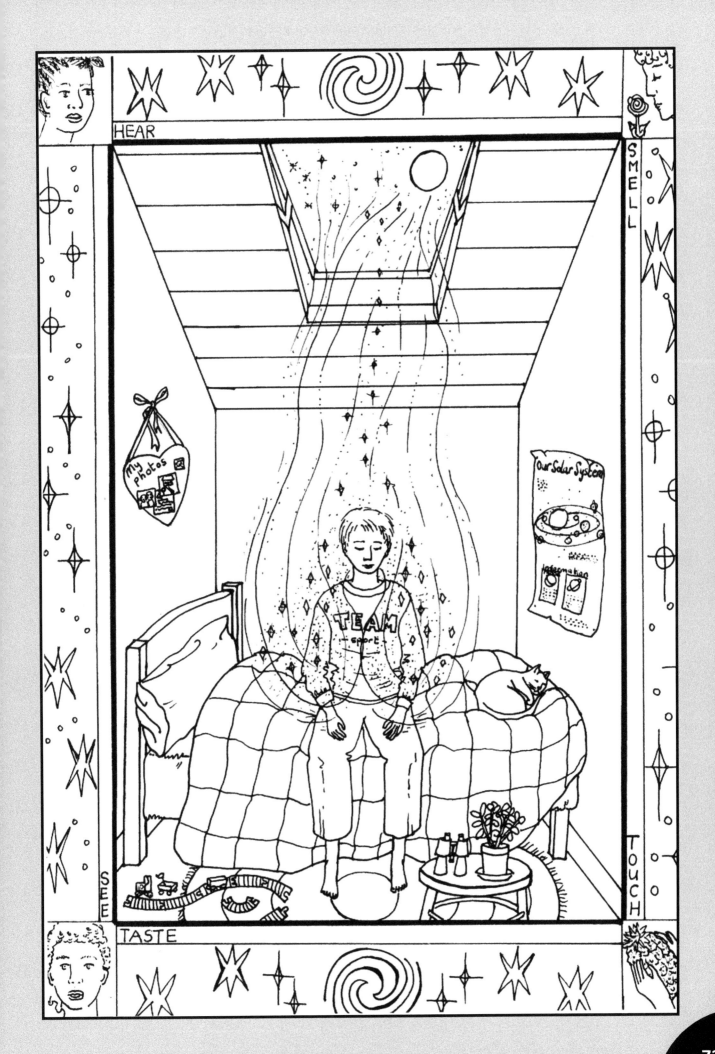

Are some of the stars in your mantle brighter than others? Their light could be particularly helpful to you; perhaps in healing an illness in your body or solving a difficulty in your life.

SEE IF YOU CAN FIND OUT WHAT THEIR LIGHT DOES.

NOW LET YOURSELF BEGIN TO NOTICE THE EDGES OF YOUR BODY,

WRIGGLE YOUR FINGERS & TOES AND WRINKLE THE END OF YOUR NOSE.

FEEL THE SOLES OF YOUR FEET, FEEL YOUR BODY IN CONTACT

WITH THE GROUND OR BED OR SEAT AND… OPEN YOUR EYES.

Once you have felt this light lit up inside you, you will never lose it.

It is always there for you to call on whenever you need it, and you can build on it whenever you repeat this exercise.

When you've got the hang of this, you can do it inside or outside – always at night.

It can be especially enjoyable at the time of the Full Moon.

DISCUSS YOUR EXPERIENCE OF THIS EXERCISE IN GROUPS & WITH YOUR TEACHER.

Additional Activities

◆ What do you think the Tibetan story of the thief is telling us?

◆ How many words can you think of, which are to do with the night? You can use the dictionary if you want.

◆ Can you remember a really beautiful night sky? Where were you? Write a short story or paint a picture to capture the feeling of that sky.

◆ Paint a picture of your starry mantle, or make one out of cloth.

18 The First-and-Last Game

a. To make a thread of connection between waking and sleeping.

b. To encourage interest in dreams and the sleep state.

First thing in the morning, just as you wake up –

NOTICE HOW YOU FEEL AND NOTICE THE ROOM YOU'RE IN.

Before you get out of bed –

STAY STILL IN BED A MOMENT, BREATHING SOFTLY.

Can you remember any dreams?

Last thing at night, as you go to sleep, see if you can

STAY AWAKE INSIDE, WHILE YOUR BODY GOES TO SLEEP.

FEEL VERY LIGHT AND PEACEFUL INSIDE YOUR TUMMY,

AND IN YOUR HEART.

Don't try too hard, or you'll stop yourself going to sleep.

Additional Activities

◆ Keep a dream notebook/diary for several months (you need to keep this by your bed, so you can write or draw as soon as you wake up).

◆ You might try describing your dreams to a good friend.

◆ Why not paint a picture of one of your dreams?

19 Wise Being

Purpose/Focus
a. To encourage responsibility.
b. To direct the child's attention to his/her true nature.

SIT VERY STILL.

CLOSE YOUR EYES AND SETTLE DOWN GENTLY INTO YOURSELF.

FEEL HOW WISE YOU ARE **when you're smiling inside, like a flower in the sun.**

IMAGINE… OR SEE… OR FEEL

YOUR WISE BEING

SITTING LIGHTLY ON TOP OF YOUR HEAD,

looking down very kindly on you and caring for you.

If you have a problem in your life or a question, the Wise Being knows what to do, and will help you if you ask with your whole heart, and with confidence that the answer or help you need will come –

SO ASK YOUR WISE BEING

IN YOUR MIND

FOR HELP WITH ANY QUESTIONS OR PROBLEMS YOU HAVE.

And now, very gently and slowly –

ALLOW YOUR WISE BEING

TO DISSOLVE INTO BRIGHT, SHIMMERING LIGHT.

…Like the rainbow that forms in the tiny crystal drops of a fine summer shower… Very, very light…

ALLOW ALL THE GOODNESS AND COLOURFUL BRIGHTNESS

TO FLOW DOWN INTO YOU THROUGH THE TOP OF YOUR HEAD,

LIKE A SWEET, WARM, SHOWER OF LIGHT.

BREATHE IT IN… DRINK IT IN…

> **As this wisdom flows into you it may even feel like a sweet nectar or healing balm.**
>
> LET THE WISDOM FILL EVERY CELL OF YOUR BODY,
>
> EVERY CORNER.
>
> LET IT FILL YOU UP COMPLETELY.
>
> **As it fills you up, it feels very soothing, very gentle and very bright. Any tight or uncomfortable places in you simply melt away. Now, your Wise Being has dissolved into you –**
>
> YOU ARE THAT WISE BEING.
>
> JUST SIT QUIETLY FOR A FEW MOMENTS.
>
> And now, gently and slowly, OPEN YOUR EYES.

You may sometimes feel a problem vanish when you do this exercise, or suddenly get a flash of inspiration which answers your question. Sometimes it won't happen immediately, but the answer will come to you later, when you're not expecting it and while you're doing something else. Maybe sometimes you won't be able to find your Wise Being. You may not be still enough, or not listening well enough, or maybe it's just not the right time to know the answer to your question.

TRY AGAIN LATER...

Additional activities

◆ Make up a song or poem about the Wise Being.

◆ Projects on famous spiritual teachers in all traditions – what did they do to stay in touch with their Wise Being all the time?

◆ What is this Wise Being?

◆ Is the Wise Being the same as, or different from, you?

◆ Where does the Wise Being come from?

◆ If someone is unhappy or telling you their problems, what does the Wise Being say about it?

Being Wise **20**

Purpose/Focus
a. To deepen and develop the previous exercise.
b. To apply the fruits of your Wise Being in life.
c. To combine the effects of several key exercises.

Perhaps you noticed during Wise Being that you were using your imagination to put the Wise Being on top of your head, and to dissolve its essence into your body at the end.

You could only do this because the Wise Being is part of you already. It is who you really are. You don't even really have to do anything to find it. When you don't try and you don't think – you are it already.

In this half of the exercise, we are not going to visualise or imagine – we are going to go to the wisdom within directly.

To do this, we are going to draw together everything we have learned and discovered by doing all the exercises so far – especially Smiling Sun Flower (page 25); Ssh! What Can you Hear? (page 28); Breathing the Sky (page 32); and Inside-Outside (page 56).

SIT QUIETLY. CLOSE YOUR EYES.
BRING YOUR ATTENTION INSIDE YOUR BODY.
FEEL THE GOOD, WARM, QUIET FEELING THAT YOU FOUND
IN SMILING SUN FLOWER, AND LET THIS GENTLE
QUALITY OF INNER SWEETNESS
E-X-P-A-N-D AND FILL YOU.
LET THE SOUNDS ENTER YOU AND PASS RIGHT THROUGH YOU, WITHOUT NAMING THEM.
NOW, BE AWARE OF THE SPACIOUS, OPEN QUALITY
THAT YOU MIGHT HAVE DISCOVERED IN SKY BREATHING.
LET ALL THESE QUALITIES BLEND INTO ONE QUALITY OF
OPENNESS, PEACE AND STILLNESS.

FORGET EVERYTHING YOU'VE DONE SO FAR;

EVERYTHING YOU'VE EVER PRACTISED; EVERYTHING YOU'VE EVER HEARD.

JUST SIMPLY BE. DO NOTHING. NO THINKING.

Thoughts might come – let them dissolve.

RETURN TO THE QUIETNESS OF BEING.

FEEL THE PURE KNOWING-NESS THAT IS YOU, NOW.

This is the wisdom of the Wise Being that you already are, when you are still and are not thinking.

LET THIS FEELING OF NATURAL WISDOM.

DEEPEN AND EXPAND,

JUST BY SITTING

AND BEING IT.

Now, without shuffling, or moving, but remaining very still and quiet –

OPEN YOUR EYES

AND LET THEM SEE WHAT IS AROUND YOU.

WHILST STILL STAYING IN TOUCH

WITH THE WISE BEING WITHIN.

You may find, from time to time, that you are in contact with this Wise Being within while you are going about your everyday activities at home and at school, and during playtimes or when talking to your friends.

Additional Activities

◆ Sharing experiences about what helps us stay in touch with this special place 'inside', and what separates us from it.

◆ Always try to respond from this place in your being.

Dedication –
To Close Your Sessions

Peace to all beings,
May all beings be well and happy,
And free from fear.

Peace to all beings.
Whether known or unknown,
Whether near or far,
Whether real or imaginary,
Whether visible or invisible,
Whether born or yet to be born.

May all beings be well and happy,
And free from fear.

Peace in all directions –
Above and below,
Through and across,
In the north,
In the south,
In the east,
And in the west.

May all beings be well and happy,
And free from fear.

Peace in all the elements –
Of earth,
And water,
And fire,
And air,
Complete in space.

May all beings be well and happy,
And free from fear.

Peace in all universes –
From the smallest cell in the body,
To the greatest galaxy in space.

Peace to all beings,
May all beings be well and happy,
And free from fear.

John Garrie, c.1972.

Resources

FOR ADULTS:

- Erricker, Clive & Jane. **Meditation in Schools** (Continuum, 2001).
- Fontana, David; Slack, Ingrid. **How to Teach Meditation to Children** (Watkins, 2007).
- Goldstein, Joseph; Kornfield, Jack. **Seeking the Heart of Wisdom** (Shambhala, 2001).
- Kabat-Zinn, Jon. **Mindfulness for Beginners** (Sounds True, 2016).
- Krishnamurti, J. **The Beginnings of Learning** (Arkana, 1990).
- Levine, Stephen. **A Gradual Awakening** (Rider, 1980).
- Long, Barry. **Meditation: A Foundation Course** (Barry Long Books, 2014).
- Long, Barry. **Raising Children in Love, Justice and Truth** (Barry Long Books, 2016).
- Rozman, Deborah. **Meditating with Children: The Art of Concentration and Centering** (Borgo Press, 1994).
- Roshi, Suzuki. **Zen Mind, Beginner's Mind** (John Weatherhill Inc, 1970).
- Thera, Nyanaponika. **The Heart of Buddhist Meditation** (Weiser, 2014).
- Tolle, Eckhart. **The Power of Now** (Hodder & Stoughton, 2001).
- Tolle, Eckhart. **A New Earth** (Michael Joseph, 2005). [this includes an excellent section on helping children deal with 'the pain body' as it manifests in moods and tantrums]
- Trungpa, Chögyam. **Shambhala: The Sacred Path of the Warrior** (Shambhala, 1984).
- Tulku, Tarthang. **Openness Mind** (Dharma Press, 1978).

FOR CHILDREN

- Delanote, Marie. **Acorns to Great Oaks** [Book & CD] (Findhorn Press, 2017).
- Kaiser Greenland, Susan. **Mindful Games** (Shambhala, 2016).
- Kluge, Nicola, Dr. **Mindfulness for Kids** (The Arts and Education Foundation, Houston, Texas, 2014).
- Snel, Eline. **Sitting Still Like a Frog** (Shambhala, 2013).
- Walsch, Neale Donald. **Conversations with God for Teens** (Hampton Roads, 2001).

ORGANISATIONS

- Children's Spirituality – https://www.childrenspirituality.org/
- Education Otherwise – https://www.educationotherwise.org/
- Human Scale Education – https://www.humanscaleeducation.com/
- Peace Prevails Education – https://peaceprevails.education/
- Religions and Environment Education Programme – https://reepinfo.org/

ABOUT THE ILLUSTRATOR

Alixandra Marschani is a primary school teacher who engages with research in early childhood and primary education to further curriculum and practices in school settings. At the heart of her work is an interest in developing innovative approaches to children's engagement with the environment, while linking nature with wellbeing.

How To Turn Your Illustrations into Stained Glass Windows

1. Trace the picture onto tracing paper.

2. Colour in the tracing paper.

3. Cut out the picture.

4. Stick it to your window!